GROUNDBREAKERS

Marie Curie

Ann Fullick

Heinemann
LIBRARY

www.heinemann.co.uk
Visit our website to find out more information about **Heinemann Library** books.

To order:
☎ Phone 44 (0) 1865 888066
📄 Send a fax to 44 (0) 1865 314091
💻 Visit the Heinemann Bookshop at www.heinemann.co.uk to browse our catalogue and order online.

First published in Great Britain by Heinemann Library,
Halley Court, Jordan Hill, Oxford OX2 8EJ
a division of Reed Educational and Professional Publishing Ltd.
Heinemann is a registered trademark of Reed Educational & Professional Publishing Ltd.

OXFORD MELBOURNE AUCKLAND
JOHANNESBURG BLANTYRE GABORONE
IBADAN PORTSMOUTH (NH) USA CHICAGO

Designed by AMR
Originated by Ambassador Litho Ltd
Printed in Hong Kong

20887
509.2

04 03 02 01 00
10 9 8 7 6 5 4 3 2 1

ISBN 0 431 10442 5

British Library Cataloguing in Publication Data
Fullick, Ann
 Marie Curie. – (Groundbreakers)
 1.Curie, Marie, – Juvenile literature
 2.Women chemists – France – Biography – Juvenile literature
 I.Title
 540.9'2

Acknowledgements
The Publishers would like to thank the following for permission to reproduce photographs:
Corbis: pp31, 34; Hulton Deutsch: p37; Mary Evans Picture Library: pp4, 5, 9, 13, 14, 20, 27, 28; Hulton Getty: pp18, 19, 23; Robert Harding Picture Library: pp17, 39; Popperfoto: pp40, 41; Science Photo Library: Jean-Loup Charmet p25, Peter Menzel p38, C Powell, P Fowler, D Perkins p26, J C Revy p24, James Stevenson p32.

Cover photograph reproduced with permission of Sipa Press.

Every effort has been made to contact copyright holders of any material reproduced in this book. Any omissions will be rectified in subsequent printings if notice is given to the Publisher.

Any words appearing in the text in bold, **like this**, are explained in the glossary.

Contents

The Polish homeland

On 7 November 1867 a Polish teacher gave birth to the last of her five children, a daughter named Marya. Madame Sklodovska had no inkling of the amazing future that lay ahead for the little girl who would always be known as 'Manya' by her parents, brother and sisters, but as Marie Curie by the rest of the world. In the late 19th century, Poland was not an easy place to live. A century before, Poland had been weak and her greedy neighbours – Germany, Russia and Austria – had **annexed** the country and divided it between them. The Poles had on several occasions tried to overthrow their oppressors, so now people such as Manya's family, who lived in Russian Poland, had a very tough existence. They were threatened with execution or banishment to Siberia if they rebelled.

Life under Russian rule

An influx of policemen, professors and minor **dignitaries** was sent from Russia to infiltrate the whole of Polish life. They watched over the population and looked out for rebellion – for example an indiscreet word or speaking Polish instead of Russian.

Polish intellectuals and teachers, like Marie Curie's father, were not allowed to think freely, and they even had to teach in Russian rather than Polish. The Catholic religion of the Poles was frowned upon, and children had to learn Russian history and Russian folk stories in school.

A busy market in 19th-century Warsaw. Polish landowners and farmers were kept poor under Russian rule.

Marie Curie in 1911. The amazing power and focus of her mind lit up her life, which she dedicated to science from beginning to end.

The scientific view of the world

Travelling back over the years to the world at the time of Marie Curie's birth, we find science that we would recognize today emerging from the **alchemists** and thinkers of the past. Charles Darwin had published his great book on evolution, *The Origin of Species*, in 1859. Faraday, Maxwell and Boltzman had moved the understanding of magnetism and electricity forward towards the modern day. And in chemistry, Dmitri Mendeleev had published his **periodic table**, the basis of the one we still use now. However many of the **elements** were still undiscovered – and this is where Marie Curie stepped in.

In a lifetime's work of sheer brilliance, Marie was to discover not one but two new elements. She would move forward the understanding of **radioactivity** immeasurably, and develop new treatments for **cancer** which are still being used.

Enter Marya Sklodovska

The girl who would be known as Marie Curie was born to lively minded and loving parents – but tragedy stalked the family. Vladislav Sklodovski was the son of a noble Polish family who, like so many others in 19th-century Poland, had fallen on hard times. He was an intellectual who taught mathematics and physics in Warsaw, the capital of Poland. His wife, a woman of great beauty and intelligence, was also a teacher and the principal of a private girls' school in Warsaw, until the birth of their children.

The couple had five children – four girls and a boy. In their early years the Sklodovski children had a comfortable home, exciting holidays in the countryside with relatives, and lots of love and attention from their devoted parents.

Early promise ...

Marie became a fluent reader at only 4 years old. In the family sitting room it was Marie who was drawn to her father's scientific instruments – the barometer, the tubes, the scales and gold leaf electroscope – like a moth to the candle-flame. As a child she had a phenomenal memory and was soon fluent in Russian as well as her native Polish. She shone in all her classes at school.

The Sklodovski children – Zosia, Hela, Marya (Marie), Joseph and Bronya – were a close-knit unit who supported each other throughout their lives.

Marie's mother, whose early death left her children with a lasting sense of responsibility for their father.

... early shadows

Little Marie was very close to her mother, and loved to spend time with her. But after the birth of her last daughter, Madame Sklodovska developed **tuberculosis** and the dreadful disease gradually took hold and spread. She never allowed herself to kiss and hug her children, in case she infected them. Often the older sisters looked after the youngest to relieve their exhausted mother.

In the autumn of 1873, Marie's father was publicly disgraced because he did not show enough respect to the Russian principal of the school in which he taught. He also lost most of his savings through poor investments. The family moved to a smaller home and took in lodgers, one of whom infected Bronya and Zosia with **typhus** in 1874. Zosia, the eldest, could not overcome the fever and died. Little Marie was only 8 when she went to her big sister's funeral.

Just two years later her beloved mother lost her fight with tuberculosis. 'I love you,' she whispered to her husband and children on her deathbed. The shadow of grief fell heavily on the little family now remaining. Young Marie learnt early that life can be very cruel.

Marie grew up rapidly, along with her brother and sisters. Her teenage years were a time for enjoying life and trying out new ideas before shouldering the burdens of responsibility and adulthood.

Bronya won a gold medal as the most outstanding pupil when she left school. So did Joseph, Marie's only brother. But while Joseph went to Warsaw University to study to become a doctor, Bronya stayed at home to look after the family, replacing the housekeepers who had run the house following their mother's death. Women were not allowed to study at Warsaw University, and so Bronya applied herself to running a happy home for her father, brother and sisters.

In Curie's words:

In this letter written by Marie Curie (aged 13) to her best friend Kazia Przyborovska, she confesses rather sheepishly to her love of school. The two girls went everywhere together.

'Do you know, Kazia, in spite of everything I like school. Perhaps you will make fun of me, but nevertheless I must tell you that I like it, and even that I love it ...'

The star pupil

Meanwhile Marie made great progress at school. She relished the experience of learning, in spite of the problems involved in being taught in Russian. Classes were a mix of Russian, Polish and German girls, many of whom, like her, were learning in a second language.

On 12 June 1883 Marya Sklodovska left secondary school – she too was awarded the gold medal for best pupil – vowing to keep in touch with all her girlhood friends for ever.

A year in the country

Marie's father decided that his youngest daughter, who had worked so hard and so well, should have a year's holiday in the countryside before deciding how she would earn her living. This is the only record we have of Marie Curie not working and simply enjoying herself for any length of time. She spent her time exploring, boating, swimming, reading – novels, not scientific texts – and going to dances and parties with her cousins and friends. At the St Louis night ball, which Marie remembered clearly all her life, she wore out a new pair of shoes dancing the night away.

Trips to balls and parties in sleighs like this were part of the magic for Marie in her year off. As she wrote to her dear friend Kazia: 'I can't believe geometry or algebra ever existed. I have completely forgotten them.'

After her year off, Marie returned to the real world with a bump, giving lessons to wealthy children to try and earn some money. At the same time she and her sister Bronya became involved in the 'Floating University', a group which provided intellectual stimulation and discussion for those too poor – or of the wrong gender – to go to university in Poland. The young people then shared their knowledge with those even poorer than themselves.

Bronya's future

Marie's brother Joseph was doing well in his training to be a doctor. Hela was unsure whether to be a teacher or a singer but was obviously going to do well at either – or both. Bronya, however, was stuck. She had run the household for four years, but what she really wanted was to go to Paris and read medicine, then return to Poland to practise as a doctor. However, there was no money to make this dream come true. Marie was particularly close to Bronya, and came up with a clever plan to make the impossible happen.

Marie's plan

At just 18 years of age Marie became a **governess** to support her elder sister at medical school. Marie was highly intelligent, and fluent in German, Russian, French, Polish and English, but she was determined that 20-year-old Bronya should have her chance. When Bronya was qualified it would be Marie's turn.

To enable Bronya to become a doctor, Marie (left) put her own ambitions aside and resigned herself to becoming a governess.

Being a governess was not as easy as Marie had thought it would be. She worked many kilometres from her beloved home and family. However, although she was homesick, she enjoyed working with the children in her care. The family treated Marie well, and after a time she began to teach the peasant children of the local village to read, helped by Bronka, the eldest daughter in her care.

First love, first heartbreak

When Casimir, the eldest son of the family, came home from Warsaw University for the holidays, he fell in love with the new, talented and attractive governess – and Marie fell in love with him. They planned to marry, but the family would not hear of it. Casimir gave in to their wishes, and Marie was heartbroken. She could not leave her job – too many people depended on her earnings – and so for another two years she stayed, nursing her sadness in the home of these people who were happy to employ her as governess, but would not consider her as a daughter-in-law. Although she did not know it at the time, this was a blessing in disguise.

The house in Poland where Marie worked as a governess for three long years.

In her years as a **governess**, Marie gave up all hope of ever studying in Paris herself. Eventually, however, things began to move in Marie's favour, though she found this hard to accept.

In 1888 Marie's father, Vladislav Sklodovski, retired. Instead of sitting and enjoying his retirement he immediately took another job at a difficult school with a very good salary and this, combined with his pension, allowed him to begin to support his family again. Bronya began to pay Marie back, so she could build up some savings.

The first chance

Then in 1890, when Bronya was very close to qualifying as a doctor, she married Casimir Dluski, who was already a doctor, and wrote to Marie asking her to come to Paris. Marie's chance had come – yet she turned it down. She felt that the family still needed her support and energies – and she was still in love with her own Casimir. She did not want to leave Poland for France and lose her chance of love.

Vladislav Sklodovski with Marie (left), Bronya and Hela in 1890, just as the family fortunes were improving a little.

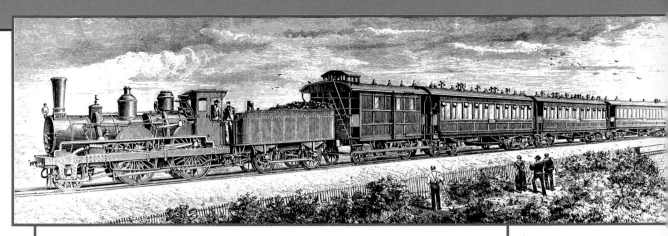

Marie sent almost everything she would need on to Paris ahead of her. Finally she hugged her father and boarded a train like this one, which would take her to Paris, to her studies and her destiny.

A second chance

While Marie was in Warsaw a very important opportunity came her way. She met up again with her friends in the 'Floating University' and this time she got the opportunity to study in a secret laboratory. Disguised from the authorities during the day as a 'museum', the laboratory was really used to teach practical science to young Poles.

Struggling to carry out experiments which she had previously only read about, Marie was gripped with a great excitement. She now knew, quite certainly, what she wanted to study – she had to be a scientist.

In spite of his parents' disapproval, Casimir and Marie stayed in touch, although he would make no commitment to her. In September 1891 they holidayed together in the mountains, where Marie finally realized this was not the man for her. Her true vocation lay in Paris, and with science. Marie could not wait to get home and write to Bronya, and she was soon on her way to Paris. Little did she guess what lay ahead of her – or that she would never live in Poland again.

In Curie's words:

'Now, Bronya ... Decide if you can really take me into your house, for I can come now. I have enough to pay all my expenses ... You can put me up anywhere ... I promise I shall not be a bore or create disorder. I implore you to answer me ...'

Within a few weeks of making her decision to go to Paris, Marie Sklodovska enrolled in the Faculty of Science at the Sorbonne, the famous Paris university, with the French version of her name – Marie rather than Marya. This was how she was known from then on.

Once Marie was established as a student she gave everything to her studies. She put no effort into socializing, so many of her fellow students did not even know her name.

When Marie first arrived in Paris she lived with Bronya and her husband Casimir Dluski in a small flat. They both worked as doctors and led a busy social life. Much as Marie loved the company, she felt that it stopped her working, so she decided to rent a tiny attic of her own, close to the university. The fact that she had no money and did not know how to cook even simple soup did not put her off.

At the Sorbonne Marie quickly realized that there were some very large gaps in her knowledge, yet she was blissfully happy, spending her days absorbed in the study of mathematics, physics and chemistry.

In Curie's words:

During her hard student days Marie wrote occasional pieces of poetry, which she kept all her life. These poems show that she actually embraced and enjoyed the hard path she had chosen:

'Ah! How harshly the youth of the student passes,
While all around her, with passions ever fresh,
Other youths search eagerly for easy pleasures!
And yet in solitude
She lives, obscure and blessed,
For in her cell she finds the ardour
That makes her heart immense.'

But not eating, and living in freezing conditions took its toll, and eventually she collapsed. Bronya and Casimir spent a week feeding her up and making her rest – and then she returned to her attic to do the same thing again.

The gifted student

Marie was not content to sit just one **Master's degree** – she worked for two; one in mathematics and the other in physics. At the same time she perfected her French until she could speak like a native. When the first year exam results were read out, all her efforts were rewarded – she was first in the year.

Marie went home for three months holiday, returning healthy, rested and plump from all the food she had been given throughout the summer. However, she returned to work and neglected herself again. In 1893 money was so tight that Marie's studies were threatened until a Polish **scholarship** ensured that her academic career was safe for the next fifteen months. Full of excitement she rushed back to Paris and her beloved laboratories.

Pierre Curie

Pierre Curie came from a close and supportive family, and he and his brother were both brilliant scientists.

In Curie's words:

Marie later reflected on her first impressions of Pierre:
'He seemed very young to me, although he was then aged thirty-five. I was struck by his clear gaze and by the slight appearance of carelessness in his lofty stature ... his smile, at once grave and young, inspired confidence.'

Marie was asked to carry out a study on the magnetic properties of various steels, but needed space to complete the work. She asked a visiting Polish professor, who invited her to tea with someone he thought might be able to help – a renowned young physicist called Pierre Curie.

The life of Pierre Curie

Pierre Curie was born in Paris on 15 May 1859. He had an older brother, Jacques, and his father and grandfather were both doctors. Pierre was a brilliant child, but he was dreamy and rather a loner. His father had a quick temper, but he was also a considerate and intelligent man. He realized that school would not suit Pierre, so he educated his son at home, allowing Pierre's mind to expand at its own rapid pace. Pierre's mother was cheerful and an expert housekeeper. The boys had a very happy childhood, full of intellectual stimulation and fun in the woodland surrounding their home.

By the time Pierre was 18 he had a **Master's degree** in physics (most students do not achieve a Master's degree until their twenties). For a number of years he and Jacques worked together, developing **piezoelectric quartz**, which allows tiny **voltages** to be measured with great precision. In 1883 the brothers reluctantly separated. Jacques became a professor at Montpellier far away in southern France, and Pierre chief of the laboratory at the School of Chemistry and Physics of the City of Paris. A few years later Pierre Curie developed an ultra-sensitive scientific scale known as the 'Curie scale'. He then discovered a fundamental law governing the relationship between temperature and magnetism, which is called 'Curie's law'.

Pierre the man

Pierre Curie was tall and a bit unruly looking with a full beard, yet he was also graceful, and quite attractive with his dark, burning eyes. However, after a disastrous early love affair he lost interest in romance – his whole focus as a young man was his work. Anything that distracted him from his physics was a nuisance, and, as he wrote in his diary: 'women of genius are rare ...'

At 35 Pierre was a successful but impoverished scientist, who seemed destined to lead a solitary life dedicated to his work. His chance meeting with Marie Sklodovska was to change all that for good.

The only distraction Pierre Curie allowed himself was a love of the countryside around Alsace in north-eastern France. Walking and cycling were passions of his, which he enjoyed during his vacations.

Love and marriage

At their first meeting, Pierre Curie and Marie Sklodovska found themselves drawn to each other. It was a meeting of two great minds and they were soon deep in conversation about physics. From this simple beginning grew one of the greatest scientific partnerships the world has ever known.

Pierre Curie was amazed by his response to Marie – he could not stop thinking about her. After several meetings he gave her a gift – a reprint of his latest publication 'On Symmetry in Physical Phenomena: Symmetry of an Electric Field and of a Magnetic Field'. He wrote on the first page: 'To Mlle (Mademoiselle or Miss) Sklodovska, with the respect and friendship of the author, P. Curie.'

Pierre was eight years older than Marie, and he was the first to declare his love. It took Marie more than a year to make up her mind. Marrying Pierre, and working with him in Paris, meant giving up for good her idea of returning to Poland to live with her father and teach. Finally, however, she could deny her feelings no longer.

When Marie Sklodovska finally agreed to marry Pierre Curie, she committed herself to a life in Paris and never lived in her native Poland again.

The wedding took place on 26 July 1895. Neither Marie nor Pierre believed in God, so they had a simple civil ceremony followed by a small gathering of their closest family and friends at the house of Pierre's parents in Sceaux near Paris. The wedding was followed by a somewhat unusual honeymoon – the Curies set off on their bicycles around the French countryside!

Monsieur and Madame Curie

Married life was a new challenge for Marie. Everything she did, she did to the best of her ability, and this was true of her marriage as well as her work. The eight or more hours of scientific research into the magnetism of steel, which she and Pierre carried out each day, were the easy part for Marie. What she found difficult was managing her household – even though it was only a tiny three-roomed flat. Marie wanted to prepare wholesome meals for Pierre, but cooking came much harder to her than physics. Her recipe books have little notes in the margins as she tried to avoid repeating mistakes!

Pierre and Marie bought their bicycles with some money given to them as a wedding present by a cousin. They used them for holidays for years to come.

In 1897 Marie Curie was expecting her first child and working on the publication of her first major research into magnetism. Her pregnancy made her ill and tired, but she refused to rest, instead setting off on the usual summer cycling trip with Pierre. Marie was very disappointed when she had to give up and go back to Paris, but on 12 September she gave birth to a healthy daughter, Irène.

A juggling act

Marie was determined that she would continue with her scientific work, as well as look after her daughter. However, she found leaving Irène with a nurse very hard, and would often rush from the laboratory just to check that the child was safe.

Life was made much easier by Pierre's father. Pierre's mother died of breast **cancer** shortly after baby Irène was born, and Pierre's father moved to live with the family. Knowing that her precious daughter was being watched over and taught by her devoted grandfather made it much easier for Marie to focus on her work.

*While Marie Curie was busy trying to combine research with family life, Antoine-Henri Becquerel was making important discoveries about **radiation**.*

The humidity and temperature in Marie's workroom changed all the time, making careful scientific measurements almost impossible. It was all that was available, however, and Marie set out to make the best of it.

ANTOINE-HENRI BECQUEREL

On 24 February 1896 Antoine-Henri Becquerel (1852–1908) was the first person to observe the natural **radioactivity** of uranium and to propose the presence of previously unknown rays. Becquerel's initial theory was that **X-rays** might be produced by fluorescent material. He was working with a uranium compound which **fluoresces** when it is exposed to sunlight. As luck would have it the sun did not shine for several days and Becquerel left his uranium sample and a photographic plate in a drawer. Eventually, when the cloudy weather showed no signs of lifting, he decided to develop the plate anyway. It was heavily fogged – radiation had been emitted by the uranium compound without the stimulation of sunlight.

A doctor's thesis

At the end of 1897 Marie had set her next target – she wanted a **doctorate**. Her imagination was caught by the findings of Becquerel (see panel). His work on the rays produced by **uranium** was so new that the field for research was wide open – ideal for working on for a doctor's thesis. Where did the energy come from and what was it made of? These were the questions which drove Marie on, and she was given the use of a closed-in, damp and crowded storeroom at the bottom of the School of Physics to begin her work.

Shut away in her damp and gloomy storeroom, Marie worked furiously. Her apparatus was not complex – she had an **ionization chamber** to show up **radiation**, a Curie **electrometer** and a **piezoelectric quartz** – but she struggled to keep everything working accurately in the poor conditions of her makeshift 'laboratory'. In spite of all the difficulties, however, interesting results soon began to emerge.

Radioactivity emerges

Firstly, Marie showed that the intensity of the radiation produced by **uranium** depended only on the amount of uranium present. The relationship between the amount of uranium and the amount of radiation was constant, and was not affected by light, temperature or the chemical state of the uranium. These results were of vital importance in showing that the radiation discovered by Becquerel really was a new and unique phenomenon, probably a property of the very uranium **atoms** themselves.

Then Marie moved on – was uranium the only **element** to possess this new property, or did other elements produce these

This page from Marie Curie's workbook was written on 6 February 1898, and shows her neat columns of figures as she recorded her results. She noted that the temperature was 6.25 °C, followed by ten exclamation marks to show her disapproval of such chilly working conditions!

Marie studied tirelessly to discover more about radioactivity.

strange rays as well? In a rush of enthusiasm she started to examine all the known chemical elements of the time. The hoped-for result was not long in coming – compounds of the element thorium also emitted rays like those of uranium. This showed that the phenomenon was not unique to uranium and needed its own name. Marie Curie suggested **'radioactivity'**.

Not content with this discovery, Marie then began to examine different **ores** and **minerals**. As she expected, only the ores of uranium and thorium showed radioactivity.

However, when she studied these minerals in detail, her results showed more radiation being given off than should have resulted from the amount of uranium or thorium present. Her first assumption was that her results were wrong, and with painstaking care she redid them all twenty times – but the results were consistently the same. Marie had already tested all the known elements for radioactivity. This new source of radioactivity, far more powerful than uranium or thorium, could only mean one thing – she had discovered a new element!

In Curie's words:

Marie and Pierre went over and over the evidence and were convinced. As Marie said to her sister Bronya: *'the radiation I couldn't explain comes from a new chemical element. The element is there and I've got to find it. We are sure! ... I am convinced I am not mistaken!'*

The new elements

Marie's early discoveries were so exciting that Pierre decided to leave his research on crystals and join his wife in her search for the new **element**. Two great scientific brains focused on the task made the work progress much faster. The couple shared observations, wrote joint papers and shared the credit for the work they performed.

Pitchblende – the uranium ore from which the Curies discovered two new elements.

The secret of pitchblende

Marie and Pierre concentrated their work on the **uranium ore pitchblende**. Bit by bit they separated it into the various elements of which it was made, and then looked for **radioactivity** in each of these elements. To their astonishment, after eliminating the uranium, they still had two sources of radioactivity. They had discovered not one but two new elements! Marie christened the first **polonium** after Poland, her beloved birthplace. The second they named **radium** – and this was the most stable, radioactive and useful of the two.

In the Curies' words:

The papers Marie and Pierre wrote at the time show how completely their work was intertwined. Although they each kept an individual laboratory notebook where they recorded the details of their experiments, they always wrote *'We found ...'* or *'We observed ...'* in their published papers, and so avoided identifying who actually did what: *'Certain **minerals** ... are very active from the point of view of the emission of Becquerel rays. In a preceding communication, one of us showed that their activity was even greater than that of uranium or thorium.'* Was it Marie or Pierre? It was their intention that no one should know.

A busy year

In 1898, the year that Marie discovered two new radioactive elements, she was also busy in her personal life. Notes in her diaries and cookbooks reveal her busy making gooseberry jelly and recording baby Irène's first steps and words.

The final proof

Some of the Curies' fellow scientists at the university did not share their belief in the new elements. To convince them that radium and polonium existed, the Curies needed to isolate the pure elements, yet they could not afford to buy the ore they needed to do this.

Marie realized that waste from the glass industry (left after uranium salts had been extracted from pitchblende) would be cheap to buy, but would still contain radium and polonium. She arranged for tons of the industrial waste to be brought from Bohemia. It then took four years (1898–1902) of hard labour in appalling conditions to melt and treat the pitchblende waste and to extract the tiny amounts of radioactive materials within.

They were utterly absorbed in their work and, at home, in their daughter. It was a time of great fulfilment and happiness for Marie Curie until finally, in 1902, she had prepared one tenth of a gram of pure radium, and determined its **atomic weight** as 225. Any doubting fellow scientists were silenced for good – radium officially existed as a newly-discovered element.

The **ionization chamber** used by Marie Curie in her search to discover the source of radioactivity.

A gift of healing

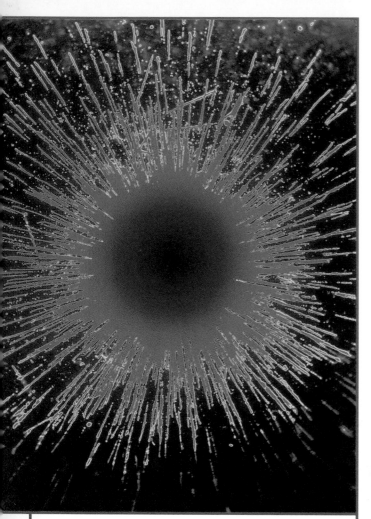

What is radium? It is an **element** which:
- gives off radiation 2 million times more intense than that of **uranium**
- gives off a gaseous substance which was known as 'emanation of radium' – now called the gas radon
- gives off heat as it decays
- makes an impression on photographic plates
- makes the atmosphere a conductor of electricity.

Radium salts are luminous – they give off light.

Radium had been the focus of the Curies' life for several years before they isolated it. During this time they also had to work as teachers at the university, to earn enough money to live on. After Pierre, in spite of his great talent, was passed over for several prestigious positions (his modesty was against him), Marie took on a teaching post at a girls' school to earn extra money. Bowed down by too much work, too little food and too much radiation, the health of the Curies began to suffer.

Family problems

Several tragedies beset the little family. Marie's beloved father died; she gave birth prematurely to a little girl, who died; and then her nephew, Bronya's son, died of tubercular meningitis. On top of this, Pierre was unwell with severe pains in his legs. Yet in spite of all these setbacks the Curies carried on working on their beloved radium.

Radium and cancer

The Curies discovered that radium 'burned' the skin, destroying the tissue. Pierre experimentally burnt his arm and watched as the skin slowly healed. They quickly recognized that radium might be used to destroy cancerous growths. **Radium therapy** (for cancer) – and the radium industry – was born.

Ernest Rutherford (left) and Frederick Soddy (right) were making many discoveries about the nature of **radioactivity** at the time when Marie Curie was doing her work on radium. Rutherford named the three types of rays – **alpha**, **beta** and **gamma radiation** – while together they developed the 'atomic disintegration theory of radioactivity'. This explains that the **nucleus** of a radioactive substance splits to form other elements and energy is released in the form of radiation.

In 1903 Marie was finally awarded the **doctorate** she so desired, and shortly afterwards she and Pierre made a momentous decision. They had developed the technique for the isolation of radium from spent **pitchblende**, and now there was a huge medical market for the rare **element**. People all over the world were clamouring for details on how to extract radium.

The Curies had a choice – they could publish their results freely for anyone to use, or they could **patent** their methods, which would limit their use and also make the Curies very wealthy. For Marie there was no choice – patenting would be contrary to the scientific spirit. In making this decision the Curies made radium treatment available to thousands, but condemned themselves to many more years of poverty and working without a proper laboratory.

Tragedy strikes

Honoured as they were to receive the Davy Medal, the Curies did not know what to do with it and gave it to their beloved six-year old Irène as a toy!

Although they did not know it, Marie and Pierre were moving towards the end of their immensely creative working partnership. Finally, after years of solitary toil, they began to be rewarded as their work was recognized by fellow scientists.

France gave Marie and Pierre Curie very little support or recognition, but other countries were more perceptive. In 1903 Lord Kelvin and the **Royal Society of London** awarded the **Davy Medal** to the Curies.

Later that same year it was announced that the **Nobel Prize** for Physics was to be split between Henri Becquerel and Marie and Pierre Curie for their work on **radioactivity**. This meant not just recognition but a very large sum of money, so Pierre could do less teaching and they could save for a proper laboratory. The money was very welcome, but the attentions of the press were not!

Only after the award of the Nobel prize did the University of Paris offer Pierre Curie a professorship of physics. He was happy to take the post, but bitter that in France recognition of their work had taken so long to come.

A beginning and an ending

In 1904 Marie and Pierre were delighted by the birth of their second daughter, Eve. Although the children were cared for by servants, to allow both parents to carry on with their work, time in the evenings and holidays was set aside to be parents and the little family was close and affectionate. Marie and Pierre relished their work together and their home life. Their marriage was truly a joining of two great minds, they were almost constant companions, and they loved each other deeply.

19 April 1906 was a wet, gloomy day. Pierre walked along the crowded, jostling streets of Paris to the laboratory, absorbed as usual in his busy thoughts. He stepped out from behind a cab to cross the road – straight into the path of a large wagon, drawn by a team of horses. The driver could not stop the wagon and the left back wheel totally crushed Pierre's skull. In that instant Pierre Curie was dead.

The devastation and grief that the death of her beloved husband brought to Marie Curie can never be measured. In one brief moment she had lost her partner in life and in work, the father of her children and her closest friend. She never fully recovered from the loss.

Pierre Curie – this was Marie's favourite portrait of her husband.

In Curie's words:

Marie recorded in her diary some of her thoughts as she sat with the body of her husband: *'Pierre, my Pierre, you are there, calm as a poor wounded man resting in sleep, his head bandaged. Your face is sweet and serene, it is still you, lost in a dream from which you cannot get out.'*

The work goes on

Marie Curie drove herself as hard as possible to do her work and bring up her two daughters, while continuing to grieve deeply for her lost partner.

In Curie's words:

Marie's diary entries after Pierre's death show her turmoil and distress:

May 11 1906: 'My Pierre, I got up after having slept rather well, relatively calm. That was only a quarter of an hour ago, and now I want to howl again – like a wild beast.'

June 10 1906: 'Everything is gloomy ...'

For some months Marie was devastated. She dressed in black, and was utterly absorbed in her loss, unable even to take comfort in her daughters. Then she was offered the chance to take over Pierre's professorship and to direct research at the School of Physics. It was the first time such a post had been offered to a woman. Full of uncertainty, she accepted.

Taking on the mantle

On Monday 5 November 1906, at 1.30 pm, Marie Curie became the first woman to deliver a lecture in the Sorbonne, the great University of Paris. She began her lecture at the precise sentence where Pierre had left off all those months before, and spoke with authority on the new theories of **radioactivity**. Thus she took up the challenge of her new life alone, supporting her family and continuing her work. Pierre's father still lived with them, helping Marie with the two little girls as she struggled to continue her work and to bring up her children.

Working on

Marie continued working with **radium** and **polonium**. She once again measured the **atomic weight** of radium and for the first and only time separated the pure metal. Radium is almost always found and used combined with other **elements** in radium salts. In order to prove that it was an element and to ensure its chemical character could be fully understood, Marie undertook this very precise work. As Curietherapy for **cancer** treatment continued to be developed, she also worked out a way of measuring minute amounts of radium by the **radiation** they produce, so that the correct doses for treatment could be calculated.

The second Nobel prize

Marie again had trouble finding recognition for her work in France when, in 1911 the Academy of Sciences refused her entry as a member. But in December of that same year the Swedish Academy of Sciences, recognizing the brilliant work Marie had done since Pierre's death, awarded her the **Nobel Prize** in Chemistry. To win one Nobel prize is the ultimate acknowledgement, to win two is unbelievable – yet Marie Curie, with her humble Polish background and constant lack of money, had done it.

In July 1914, three years after Marie was awarded her second Nobel prize, the Institute of Radium was opened in Paris. It was known as the Pavillon Curie and was built on rue Pierre Curie. At last Marie had the laboratory that she and Pierre had dreamed of – it was just far too late for them to share it.

Not long after Marie Curie was awarded her second **Nobel prize** her health failed her badly. She had to have surgery on her kidneys and took a long time to recover. She recuperated, spending time with her daughters and a group of friends, including Albert Einstein (the physicist who became world famous when he developed the **theory of relativity**) and his son. Einstein and Marie Curie spent hours discussing ideas – some of them forming the beginning of Einstein's groundbreaking work.

By 1914 Marie's life was more stable. The girls were growing up – Irène was 17 and Eve was 10, the Curie Institute had been opened, her research was going well and she had rented a villa in Brittany for the summers. But a new cloud was building on the horizon – the outbreak of World War 1.

The outbreak of war

When the war broke out Marie recognized that **X-rays**, which she had studied closely, could be vital in helping to treat

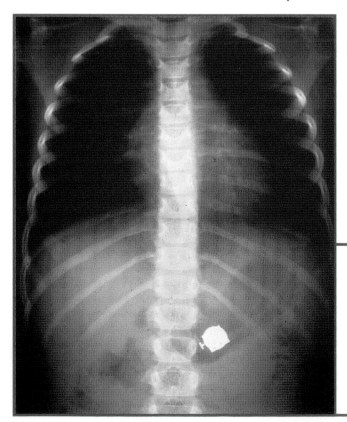

wounded soldiers – being an excellent tool for finding foreign objects, such as bullets and pieces of shrapnel lodged in the body. First she organized moving all available X-ray apparatus from laboratories to hospitals, but rapidly realized that the equipment was really needed out in the field.

X-rays are of enormous value in identifying broken bones, and they also show up any foreign body such as a bullet or an object that has been swallowed by accident. The person in this X-ray has swallowed a wrist watch.

Marie Curie in 1914, at the wheel of the Renault which she converted into her first 'radiological car'.

The 'radiological car'

It did not take Marie long to solve the problem of getting X-ray equipment out to the troops where it was needed. She took an ordinary car and fitted it with Röntgen apparatus (see below) and a **dynamo**, which could be driven by the engine of the car, to power the X-ray machine.

As the war progressed into a long and bloody conflict, Marie organized the manufacture and equipping of twenty of these radiological cars, which were then sent to the front line. Known as 'little Curies', they carried the X-ray equipment to the field hospitals full of injured and dying men.

Marie also set up 200 radiological rooms at field hospitals, and these made it possible for over a million wounded men to be examined. She drove herself relentlessly, as always, only returning home when she was ill herself.

WILHELM RÖNTGEN

In 1895 Wilhelm Konrad Röntgen (1845–1923) was investigating materials that **fluoresce** when they are exposed to **cathode rays**. In doing his work he discovered new rays which also caused fluorescence, but which penetrated the paper and metal that stopped the cathode rays. Röntgen had discovered X-rays and, within days of his announcement, doctors began to use them to see inside the human body without cutting it open.

Winning the two **Nobel prizes** had given Marie Curie enough money to live and work without concern. But during the war she ploughed all of her money into the French war effort, and lost it all. When peace was restored, funding for research became a worry once more. However, help was to come from an unexpected direction.

An American benefactor

Mrs William Brown Meloney was editor of a prestigious New York magazine and well known in American society. For years she had wanted to meet Marie Curie and eventually a brief interview was organized. What Mrs Meloney discovered, to her complete astonishment, was that Marie Curie's new laboratory had little or no equipment and only 1 gram of **radium**, which was used solely for the treatment of **cancer**. America, on the other hand, had about 50 grams of radium. Marie Curie needed a gram of radium to continue her research, but she could not afford the $100,000 needed to buy it ...

In Mrs Meloney's words:

Mrs Meloney was completely overawed when she finally met Marie Curie. In an account she wrote afterwards she said: *'My timidity exceeded her own. I had been a trained interrogator for twenty years, but I could not ask a single question of this gentle woman ... I tried to explain that American women were interested in her great work and found myself apologizing for intruding on her precious time ...'*

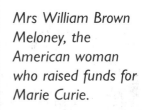

Mrs William Brown Meloney, the American woman who raised funds for Marie Curie.

A visit to America

Mrs Meloney went home inspired, and determined that she and the women of America would do something to help. She launched the Marie Curie Radium Fund in all the major cities of America, and in less than a year the money had been raised. She invited Marie to come to America with her daughters to receive her radium. It was a measure of Marie's gratitude to America that at the age of 54 she undertook the longest journey of her life.

In America, Marie was constantly surrounded by people. She appreciated the concern and support of her American friends but found it almost more than her fragile constitution could bear. At the end of the visit Marie was exhausted, but content. She felt that she had contributed to the friendship between America, France and Poland; that she had won many hearts and gained a lifelong friend in Mrs Meloney; and she also had her precious radium.

In 1921 Marie Curie received a gram of radium from the president of the United States himself, Warren G. Harding.

After the success of the trip to America, Marie continued her work with **radium**. From the end of the war she had been aided by her daughter Irène and, from 1926, Irène's husband Frédéric Joliot joined them. The three of them took great pleasure in working together, sharing ideas along with family life.

Failing health

As a young student Marie Curie had eaten poorly and made herself ill. Once she started working on **radioactivity**, she took no precautions, handling her beloved radium with bare hands and unshaded eyes. Even when it had become apparent that the **element** caused burns, and other workers were beginning to protect themselves by using gloves and goggles, Marie refused to let anything come between her and the radium she loved. As she got older, she began to pay the price of her pioneering work.

In 1923 she was threatened with blindness, when cataracts took her sight, but surgery restored her vision. The damage to her internal organs could not be rectified so easily.

Marie and her daughter Irène took great pleasure in working together, just as Marie and Pierre had done.

The face of Marie Curie in old age reflects the hard work and sadness that filled much of her life. She gave a great deal, and took very little.

Last days

In 1934 Marie left her beloved laboratory for the last time, feeling dreadfully ill. Her health went into a downward spiral from which there was no return. Increasingly weak and tired, with high fevers and pain, doctors could not decide what was wrong with her. She was sent to a sanatorium in the mountains, where her devoted younger daughter Eve nursed her as the number of white and red cells in her blood plummeted. Finally, at dawn on 4 July 1934, Marie Curie gave up the battle for life. The doctor who had cared for her reported that she died of 'an aplastic pernicious **anaemia** of rapid, feverish development. The bone marrow did not react, probably because it had been injured by a long accumulation of **radiations**.' Marie's precious radium was the cause of her death. At the relatively young age of 67 she was buried with her beloved Pierre, in the family tomb at Sceaux. Her life's work was over.

IRÈNE AND FRÉDÉRIC JOLIOT-CURIE

Irène and Frédéric Joliot-Curie formed another close-knit husband and wife team. Working in the Institute of Radium, the Joliot-Curies were the first people to develop an artificial radioactive element – a radioactive form of phosphorus. This work won them the **Nobel Prize** for Chemistry in 1935. In 1939 they demonstrated that the fission (splitting) of **uranium** can lead to a **chain reaction**, a discovery which has had a major effect both on the development of nuclear weapons and of nuclear power.

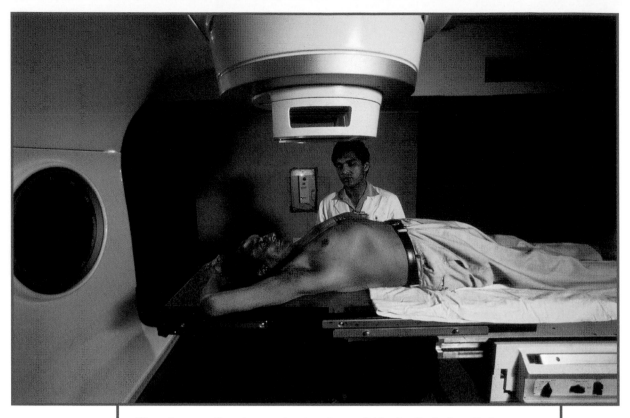

The therapy first begun in the time of Marie Curie is still, in a more sophisticated form, saving lives today.

The **radium** which Marie and Pierre Curie isolated with such painstaking care, and the work that Marie continued to do on her own into the nature of **radioactivity**, left a long-term legacy from which we still benefit today.

The **cancer** treatment they developed will continue to save lives well into the 21st century. Curietherapy has been refined and developed a great deal, but radiotherapy using radium is still very important in the treatment of cancers. Methods of delivering the radioactivity to exactly the right place are improving all the time. Other radioactive materials can be used to trace pathways in the body and to help doctors treat a wide variety of conditions without having to resort to surgery.

The pioneering work of Marie Curie has also led to a wide range of applications beyond the field of medicine, where radium and other radioactive **elements** are so widely used.

Food preservation

For centuries the main methods of preserving food remained the same – salting, drying, cooling and pickling. More recently freezing and canning were developed. Late in the 20th century another new method of food preservation was discovered – irradiation. If food is exposed to a low dose of **radiation**, the bacteria and mould spores on it are killed off very effectively, prolonging the life of the products considerably. This is a big advantage to the people selling the food, but there has been some resistance from consumers who felt they were getting little benefit and perhaps some increased risk.

Electricity can be generated in a nuclear power station using a controlled chain reaction.

Electricity without strings?

Irène and Frédéric Joliot-Curie carried on and extended the work they started with Marie Curie to show that when **uranium** decays it can set up a **chain reaction**. If the energy produced in that chain reaction is controlled, it can be used to drive turbines and make electricity in a nuclear power station.

As the 21st century begins, people all over the world are becoming increasingly dependent on electricity. Yet most of the traditional methods of producing electricity depend on burning fossil fuels. This raises two large problems – it creates a lot of pollution and fossil fuels will not last for ever. In an ideal world nuclear power would be the clean and pollution-free way to make electricity. It has not yet worked out like this however, as radioactive waste causes problems of its own. But, as reserves of fossil fuels get used up, nuclear power may be of enormous importance in the future.

The 'mushroom cloud' over Nagasaki after the dropping of an atomic bomb. When the bombs were dropped no one knew for sure how much energy would be released, or what the effects would be. Only when the 'mushroom clouds' had died away and the war was over, could the effect of these experimental bombs be measured.

Marie Curie recognized that, while the work she was doing held great potential for good, there was also the possibility that the power she had discovered could be used for evil purposes.

The work started by Marie, and continued by her daughter Irène and her husband, had led to a rapidly growing understanding of **radioactivity** and what happens in a **chain reaction**. During World War II fears grew that Nazi Germany would use this knowledge to develop a nuclear weapon. This resulted in the setting up of the Manhattan project, to develop a nuclear weapon for the Allies. Although the war with Germany ended in May 1945, the war with Japan continued. In August 1945, the only atomic bombs ever to be used in warfare were dropped on the Japanese cities of Hiroshima and Nagasaki. The Japanese surrendered on 2 September 1945 and World War II was over.

Brighter than a thousand suns

The atomic explosions were devastating. The light seared the eye-balls and blinded those who saw it. People were literally **vaporized**. Thousands more died in the following days from severe burns and acute **radiation** sickness. For years to come yet more people died from the type of **anaemia** that had killed Marie Curie herself, and from **cancers** triggered by the massive radiation doses they had received. Women gave birth to babies with severe genetic defects, caused by the effects of radiation, and many other children developed cancers which were linked to the radiation their parents had been exposed to. Scientists are still collecting evidence on the long-term effects of the dropping of those two nuclear bombs.

A shadow over the future

During the **Cold War** between the former Soviet Union and the West in the 1960s, 70s and 80s, fears of war and of the sabotage of nuclear power stations were high. This led to billions of pounds, dollars and roubles being spent on stockpiles of nuclear weapons, with the capacity to destroy the whole planet many times over. Although the threat of the Cold War has been largely lifted with the fall of the Berlin wall in 1989, and the break-up of the former Soviet block, fear of nuclear weapons in the wrong hands is one legacy from the work of Marie Curie which is unlikely ever to leave us.

This US nuclear missile, the Titan II, was built in 1963, at the height of the Cold War. It was capable of flying over 8000 km (5000 miles) and of crossing the Atlantic.

Even though the Curie family was spread through Poland, Austria and France, the bond between Marie (left) and her brother and sisters was strong, and they remained closely involved in each other's lives.

Marie Curie travelled a very long way in her lifetime. From her beginnings in oppressed Poland, she became one of the greatest scientists of her time. Her discoveries rank with the greatest, and her work is still of enormous relevance.

Marie's early childhood was happy if hard. She had loving parents, and sisters and a brother with whom she played and enjoyed all the pleasures of family life. Although they had their share of tragedies, with the loss of both their eldest sister and their mother, the family was close-knit and supportive of each other throughout their lives.

A finely focused mind

Once Marie moved to Paris and began her studies she showed the most remarkable focus on her work. Her determination to study and shine in the sciences led her to ignore almost everything else. Her dedication was rewarded however, not only in the amazing discoveries she was to make, but also in the deep love she shared with her husband, Pierre Curie.

Their incredible discovery of two new radioactive **elements** was all the more astonishing because of the dreadful conditions in which they had to work. It was the supreme tragedy of Marie's life that Pierre was killed while they were still relatively young. Although she continued her work, which could scarcely have been more impressive if Pierre had lived, she carried at all times a deep sadness over his loss.

A scientist of genius

The stature of Marie's work on **radioactivity** can be measured in the fact that she was awarded not one, but two **Nobel prizes** – and this at a time when women were rarely liberated from their roles as housewives and mothers. Marie proved that it was possible to combine motherhood with a brilliant career. She fulfilled all of her academic promise and died while still engaged in her work, her body destroyed by the **radiation** with which she had spent so much of her life. She was one of the greatest scientists of all time.

The legacy of Marie Curie lives on in medicine, in power-generation and industry, and in weapons of war. She was a woman of genius.

Timeline

1859	Pierre Curie is born on 15 May in France.
1867	Marya Sklodovska (later Marie Curie) born on 7 November in Warsaw, in Russian-occupied Poland.
1873	Marie's father loses his savings after poor investments.
1878	Her mother dies of **tuberculosis.**
1879	The scientist Albert Einstein is born in Germany.
1883	Marie leaves secondary school with honours – she is awarded the gold medal for best pupil.
1885–88	Marie works as a **governess**.
1891	Goes to Paris to study science.
1893	Meets Pierre Curie.
1895	Marries Pierre Curie.
	Wilhelm Röntgen discovers **X-rays**.
1896	Henri Becquerel demonstrates that **uranium** salts emit rays of an unknown nature without exposure to light.
1897	Marie and Pierre's first daughter, Irène is born.
1898	Marie discovers two new **radioactive elements** – **polonium** and **radium.**
1903	Awarded a **doctorate.**
	Marie and Pierre are awarded the **Davy Medal** by the **Royal Society of London**, and the **Nobel Prize** for Physics, together with Henri Becquerel.
1904	Marie and Pierre's second daughter, Eve, is born.
1906	19 April Pierre Curie is killed in a traffic accident in Paris.
	5 November Marie becomes the first woman to deliver a lecture at the Sorbonne, the University of Paris.
1911	Marie is awarded the Nobel Prize for Chemistry.
1914	The Institute of Radium – the Pavillon Curie – opens in Paris.
1914–18	World War I. Marie organizes 'radiological cars' to examine soldiers by X-ray in the field.
1918	Marie's daughter Irène starts to work with her mother.
1921	The American Marie Curie Radium Fund raises the $100,000 needed to buy Marie 1 gram of radium, and she travels to America to receive it.
1926	Irène's husband, Frédéric Joliot, starts to work with Marie and Irène.

1934	4 July Marie Curie dies of **cancer** caused by **radiation.**
1935	Irène and Frédéric Joliot-Curie win the Nobel Prize for Chemistry for producing the first artificial radioactive substances.
1945	Two atomic bombs dropped on the Japanese cities of Hiroshima and Nagasaki.

Places to visit and further reading

Places to visit

The Curie Institute in Paris, France

The Science Museum, South Kensington, London, UK – houses a number of Curie artefacts, as well as a gallery on radioactivity and nuclear power. The museum's website at www.nmsi.ac.uk has links to an online exhibition on Marie Curie.

The Nobel Foundation website at www.nobel.se has information about the Nobel prize and those who have won it.

Further reading

Macdonald, Fiona: *The World in the Time of Einstein* (Belitha Press, London, 1998)

Parker, Steve: *Marie Curie and Radium* (Belitha Press, London, 1994)

Tames, Richard: *Hiroshima* – Turning Points in History series (Heinemann Library, Oxford, 1998)

Wallace, Karen: *Marie Curie* (Franklin Watts, London, 1998)

Glossary

alchemist people who experimented with metals in the Middle Ages – in particular they tried to turn base metals into gold and discover the elixir of life

alpha rays radiation consisting of alpha particles i.e. helium nuclei

anaemia a lack of red blood cells

annex take over by force

atom the smallest particle of an element

atomic weight combined value of the protons and the neutrons in the nucleus of an atom – now called the atomic mass or nucleon number

beta rays radiation consisting of streams of beta particles or electrons

cancer the uncontrolled growth of cells to form a tumour

cathode rays high energy electrons

chain reaction nuclear reaction where the neutrons produced by the splitting of one atom cause the splitting of more atoms, and the neutrons from this cause further fissions (splittings) so the reaction becomes self-sustaining

Cold War a time of unfriendly relations (but no actual warfare) between the US and communist countries

Davy Medal one of the highest awards given by the Royal Society in memory of the scientist Sir Humphry Davy

dignitary important person

doctorate higher degree, e.g. a Doctor of Philosophy (PhD) or a Doctor of Science

dynamo device for producing electrical energy from mechanical energy

electrometer apparatus for measuring voltage

element a substance made up of only one type of atom

fluoresce give off visible light in response to exposure to ultraviolet light, for example sunlight

gamma rays very penetrating radiation

governess someone who teaches the children of a family at their own home – often living with the family as well

ionization chamber special chamber which allows ionizing radiation to be detected

Master's degree degree taken after a first ordinary or honours degree. May be the result of research, or a taught degree.

minerals substances found in rocks

Nobel prize awarded by the Nobel Foundation in memory of the Swedish scientist and inventor Alfred Nobel. Awarded for outstanding achievement in physics, chemistry, medicine, literature, economics and for the promotion of world peace. The prize includes a substantial sum of money – today it is around £850,000.

nucleus central part of an atom containing protons and neutrons. The nucleus of an atom contains virtually all of its mass.

ore compound of a metal found in rocks – the metal can be extracted from the ore

patent permission granted by a government to allow an inventor to make, use and sell an invention for a set period of time. Anyone else wishing to use that procedure or invention has to pay the original inventor.

periodic table way of arranging the chemical elements according to the numbers of electrons in their atoms

piezoelectric quartz a crystal which distorts when a voltage is applied to it

pitchblende uranium ore

polonium first radioactive element discovered by Marie Curie – named after Poland

radiation (ionizing) particles or rays given off by radioactive nuclei

radioactivity emission of radiation by a nucleus as it decays

radium one of the radioactive elements discovered by Marie Curie

radium therapy treatment for cancer using the radiation from radium to destroy cancer cells

Royal Society of London very prestigious academic society

scholarship money granted to a student to cover their educational costs

theory of relativity suggests that all motion can only be measured relative to something else and therefore nothing is absolute

tuberculosis bacterial disease widespread in the 19th and early 20th century, which affected many parts of the body but particularly the lungs; often known as TB

typhus infectious fever characterized by a purple rash, headaches and fever

uranium radioactive element

vaporized turned into a vapour

voltage measure of electric force

X-ray ray of very short wavelength which can penetrate matter too dense for light-rays to pass through, for example skin